Buttermilk Pie!

Copyright © 2022 Lula Jane's LLC

All rights reserved. No part of this publication may be reproduced, distributed, or transmitted in any form or by any means, including photocopying, recording, or other electronic or mechanical methods, without the prior written permission of the publisher, except in the case of brief quotations embodied in critical reviews and certain other noncommercial uses permitted by copyright law. For permission requests, write to the publisher at the following email address: lulajanes@gmail.com

ISBN: 979-8-218082-72-7 (Hardcover)
ISBN: 979-8-218082-73-4 (eBook)

Buttermilk Pie!

SECRETS FROM LULA JANE'S

Nancy Grayson

Photography by Chris McSwain

Project Manager Sinai Wood

Lula Jane's

SWEETS

- PIES -
- Big Mama's Buttermilk Pie 3^{50}
- Peanut Butter Crunch Pie 4^{00}
- Cream Pies 4^{00}
- Lemon Chess 3^{50}
- Fudge Pie 3^{50}
- Blueberry Pie 4^{50}
- Key Lime 3^{50}
- French Silk 5^{20}

- CAKES -
- Chocolate Dirty Cake 4^{00}
- Pearl White Cake 4^{00}
- Pound Cake 3^{00}

- COOKIES AND MORE -
- Chocolate Chip 1^{50}
- Oatmeal Raisin 1^{50}
- Peanut Butter 1^{50}
- Oatmeal Chocolate
- Sgt. Butter 1^{50}
- People Cookies 1^{50}
- Mocha Iced Brownies 3^{00}
- Bread Pudding

Table of Contents

1	Introduction
7	Caveats
9	Ingredients Matter

BREAKFAST

15	Baked Oatmeal
17	Banana Bread
19	Biscuits
21	Biscuits - Quick & Easy
22	Breakfast Bar
23	Breakfast Cookie
25	Breakfast Pie
27	Cinnamon Rolls
31	Scones - Cranberry-Orange
33	Scones - Savory
34	Zucchini Bread

LUNCH & DINNER

38	Hummus
39	Pimiento Cheese
40	Potato-Corn Chowder
43	Power Bowl
47	Quesadillas
49	Quiche
53	Tomato Pie

SWEETS

57	Blueberry Pie
58	Bread Pudding
59	Brownies
63	Buttermilk Pie
65	Buttermilk Pound Cake
67	Carrot Cake
68	Cherry Pie
69	Chocolate Chip Cookies
73	Chocolate Cake
75	Coconut Cream Pie
79	French Silk Pie
83	Fudge Pie
84	German's Chocolate Cake
87	Italian Cream Cake
91	Key Lime Pie
93	Oatmeal Chocolate Chip Cookies
94	Oatmeal Raisin Cookies
95	Peanut Butter Crunch Pie
97	Pecan Pie
98	Pumpkin Pie
99	Red Velvet Cake
101	White Cake
103	Wicked Pie

ETC.

108	Caramel Sauce
109	Chocolate Buttercream Frosting
110	Cream Cheese Frosting
111	White Buttercream Frosting
112	Lemonade and Iced Tea
113	Pie Crust
116	Comeback Sauce
116	Avocado-Cilantro Dressing
116	Garlic-Parmesan Sauce
117	Champagne Vinaigrette Dressing
118	Woofies (Dog Treats)
121	Index

Introduction

Being southern frames food for me. The southern table has been a place that provided communication, connections, and respect—a space for joy and an appreciation of fresh food. Conversations were lively but cloaked in decorum so that individual ideas were valued. My grandmother's kitchen always smelled of rising yeast rolls and chicken frying. Truth be known, Lula Jane was not a great cook but instead had a cook who came in daily—and she was a marvel.

Daily life was Decatur, Georgia, with holidays in Mississippi (think Pelahatchie, Gulde, Edwards, etc.). I remember fresh milk left on the doorstep in the morning with the cream rising to the top, running down the road for freshly churned butter, and porch sitting while snapping beans or shucking corn. My connection to the source of food and the great food on the table was strong. I know firsthand how important the best and freshest ingredients are. At the time, I am sure I had no idea how privileged I was!

I also recall catching "lightning bugs" as a child, dropping them into a Coke bottle, and briefly enjoying the natural, magical "light" as dusk set in. It was a combination of curiosity, experimentation, and joy. That same combination, for me, is what baking is really about.

I also believe individuals can morph at any time—a favorite phrase of mine. Morphing equates with becoming, growing, changing to adapt, changing to evolve, and becoming something that our past has prepared us for. I have always seen my life as a system of paths that initially appear unconnected, but then somehow connect to form a morphing experience for me. Life has afforded me opportunities that I do not take for granted. I have been privileged by these opportunities—these were doors that opened, and I risked stepping through. Let me assure you, I am no chef—I've never been to culinary school – not ashamed to say that I am self- taught and an eager learner.

There are a few reasons why I'm writing this cookbook—perhaps goals that are unusual.

I owned a bakery for nine years—with some acclaim and recognition. I don't believe that a bakery should be about sugar and sweetness. Food should taste like fine ingredients. Covering everything with lots of sugar is something anyone can do. Get a different cookbook for that!

Everyone kept asking for my recipes. When you have a bakery, your recipes are what make you successful. After nine years, I closed the restaurant, not because of lack of demand or success, but because in the wake of the pandemic it became too much of a struggle to hire enough staff to meet the increasing demands. The community was distraught and asked that I teach cooking classes. I believe this is my time to retire. Thus, I want to write recipes in a way that will help folks actually make what they tasted and loved at Lula Jane's in Waco. Our customers don't want to just make bakery goods, they want to be able to make the great-tasting bakery goods and meals that we served.

Baking isn't difficult, it is practiced, it is experimental, and it is an expression of who you are and what you like: flavors, texture, appearance. Baking is the gift you give of yourself, your time, and your skill. Recipes are just starters—you amend them to make them your own. Embrace the mistakes and celebrate them as opportunities to become a better baker or cook.

I want you to become a happy baker!

INTRODUCTION

MY INCREDIBLE PARTNERS

Want the best? Build a strong team. Together we have woven an amazing cookbook. Sinai Wood has been the tech-savvy, forward movement, editing motivator—a real gift to this project. Elizabeth Vardaman graciously and somewhat tentatively suggested edits—always with apologies where apologies were not needed. She has a keen eye for wording, thank goodness. Chris McSwain used her magic to make the food come to life with inspired photography. Whether it was food or surroundings, it feels like you are stepping into the scene—as if you are there! And a big thanks to the friends and relatives who used the recipes to actually make the real food—testing the clarity of the recipes.

Sinai Wood: Associate Professor and Documents Librarian, Baylor University.

Elizabeth Vardaman: Associate Dean for Special Programs, College of Arts and Sciences (National & International Scholarship Programs), Retired, Baylor University.

Chris McSwain: Family and commercial photography—a graduate of LSU.

And then there are staff members over the years. Some knew and understood the world of baking and cooking, some came to learn and develop as "greats" in the kitchen. All were eager and inspired to contribute and become. I treasure these friendships and always enjoy their return visits.

To my family, husband of over 50 years + two amazing daughters—I thank you for always being there when life was tough.

NOT MY RECIPE

I so respect the integrity of those who have worked hard on recipes. To honor these folks, I readily admit to using particular recipes at Lula Jane's that provided outstanding products. Here I list those recipes that our customers want—and sources where they can find them:

Iced Butter Cookies—*Pastry Queen*—Rebecca Rather
Beet Burgers—*The Happy Pear*—David & Stephen Flynn

CAVEATS

There are always different ways to make foods. I'm simply offering those recipes that have worked for me and that have drawn customers ...

Good is never good enough—always seek better in a quest toward excellence. My theory is that I can never reach excellence, so I continue to tweak recipes as they morph toward better and better.

Trial and error is the best way—don't be afraid to fail, failure is our best teacher. Always acknowledge mistakes and failures so that you are driven not to repeat them as "good enough."

Then there is chemistry—all baking and cooking is chemistry. When you amend a recipe, take into account pH, heat, balance, measurement, etc.

Baking and cooking require ingredients AND process. Sometimes one is more important than another—so pay attention. Don't assume that you already know how to make something. READ THE RECIPE ALL THE WAY THROUGH.

Ingredients matter. The quality of the outcome is only as good as the components you use.

How you put those pieces together can make a huge difference in the outcome of whatever you are making. One of my most important lessons is that a mixer cannot thoroughly incorporate whatever is in the bottom of the bowl. It always takes some degree of muscle to stir by hand in order to insure an even mix.

INGREDIENTS MATTER

The end product is dependent on the quality of the ingredients. This is a tough call because of cost, accessibility, allergies, and taste preferences. I will attack these problems from the standpoint of having your end product come out as close to Lula Jane's as possible.

BUTTER: This is SO important—as there is a huge variance in the percentage butter fat content across brands and not usually listed on the package. You will have to do your homework with companies to get this information. I try to always approximate 85% butter fat content. You can absolutely tell the difference in the taste of the end product. I also **use only unsalted** butter as it allows me to control the salt in each recipe.

Kerrygold and Falfurrias butters generally have higher butter fat content than other brands or store brands.

CINNAMON: The region where cinnamon grows (tree bark) has an impact on the oil content and flavor. I no longer keep regular cinnamon—but prefer to use the more flavorful Vietnamese. You can actually smell the difference when you open the container. Specialty cinnamons are available on line, in the baking area of your grocery, or order from Southern Specialty Spices in Austin, TX.

MILK: I only keep and use whole milk, half-and-half, and heavy cream. You can experiment with lower fat milks for healthy recipes...just realize that this will change the outcomes in flavor and texture.

BUTTERMILK: Use real buttermilk. Rather than shaking the container before you pour and measure, simply roll the container back and forth a few times. If you shake it, you are adding air bubbles and this changes the measurement. Also, these recipes aren't the same if you try to substitute using milk and an acid (vinegar / lemon juice / etc).

VANILLA: Always use the real deal—no imitation extracts ever. There is such a great variance in the richness of vanilla extract and you can tell when you smell it. I have found a marvelously rich vanilla from Mexico which someone transports for me from Galveston, TX. Because Mexico does not regulate their products/ingredients, there is an even greater difference among those available. Overall, just realize that buying vanilla really is a "crap shoot"!

Flours: When these recipes call for "flour", the reference is for all purpose flour. I use Gold Medal because all of my recipes are tested with this. If you select another brand or a store brand, the outcome will vary somewhat. All flours are not the same in grind or type.

Cake flour is sometimes difficult to find. It often comes in a box rather than bagged.

Wheat flour is a 100% wheat flour in these recipes. It adds a somewhat nutty flavor and has a different moisture content than all purpose flour.

Breakfast!

Baked Oatmeal

My goal with the oats was to provide a healthy breakfast option daily. The huge demand for the oatmeal was a real surprise. It is loved by all ages - and I admit folks offered money for this recipe (which I never did!).

PREHEAT OVEN TO 350 DEGREES

8 X 8 BAKING PAN 6 SERVINGS	9 X 13 BAKING PAN 12 SERVINGS
1 1/2 bananas	3 bananas
1 c blueberries (fresh or frozen)	2 c blueberries (fresh or frozen)
2 c old fashioned oats	4 c old fashioned oats
2 T brown sugar	4 T brown sugar
1/2 t salt	1 t salt
1 t baking powder	2 t baking powder
1 1/2 t Vietnamese cinnamon	1 T Vietnames cinnamon
1/2 c chopped pecans or walnuts	1 c chopped pecans or walnuts
1 egg	2 eggs
1 1/2 t vanilla	1 T vanilla
2 T unsalted butter melted	1/4 c unsalted butter melted
2 c whole milk warmed	4 c whole milk warmed

OATS: old fashioned not steel cut / not quick cook. I use Quaker Oats. Spray the baking pan—sides and bottom.

Slice bananas about 1/8" thick and spread evenly in pan. Spread the blueberries on top.

In bowl mix well: oats, brown sugar, salt, baking powder, cinnamon and nuts. Spread this dry mix on top of blueberries & bananas.

Warm milk in microwave in a glass measuring cup until warm to touch (95 seconds). While warming, lightly whisk together egg(s), vanilla & melted butter—and mix in the warmed milk.

Pour the liquid mixture over the oats.

Bake for 30 min.

SERVING SUGGESTIONS: top baked oatmeal with brown sugar, melted butter, milk and whipped cream.

STORING: refrigerate and use for a couple more days or wrap cut squares individually in plastic wrap and freeze. Oatmeal any time you want it: place in bowl and microwave until hot.

Banana Bread

So many banana bread recipes so you have to try several to find the one that suits your taste. This one is flavorful and moist, and is my personal favorite. See what you think.

1 LOAF

PREHEAT OVEN 350

2 c flour
1 t baking soda
1/4 t salt
1 egg
1 rounded cup sugar
1/2 cup oil
2 T buttermilk
1 t vanilla
3 ripe bananas mashed well
1/2 c chopped nuts + extra for sprinkling on top (optional)
Spray and flour loaf pan.

Set aside well-mixed flour, soda & salt. Mix bananas, vanilla & buttermilk in a separate bowl.

Using a stand mixer and paddle, combine egg, sugar & oil. Add 1/2 the flour mix. Add 1/2 banana mix…being careful to hand-stir the bottom of the mixing bowl several times. Repeat with flour & banana. Be sure to mix well with spatula to get all batter from the bottom of the mixer before pouring into the pan.

Add nuts and mix. Pour into pan & sprinkle top lightly with nuts.
Bake 1 hr 20 min.

Biscuits

These biscuits have incredible rise and flakiness. And the bonus in learning to make these is that it is also the recipe and technique for our amazing savory scones! In working the butter into the flour, I have tried all the techniques: frozen butter, cold butter, grating butter, chopping butter, using a food processor...you name it, I've tried it. So this recipe gives my personal favorite technique with great results.

Yes—you can make GREAT biscuits—show stoppers!

3 3/4 cup + 2 T flour • 2 T baking powder • 1 t salt
1 c room temp unsalted high quality butter
2 c cold heavy whipping cream • extra flour for dusting

Whisk the flour, baking powder and salt really, really well. The dry ingredients should be fully mixed. Drop the whole chunk of room temp butter into this mix.

I wear gloves for the rest of the process because it is a real mess! Grab the butter and under/within the flour mix, mush the butter into the flour.

Continue this process to introduce flour into butter pieces as you mush it into smaller pieces. You want to end up with butter pieces that aren't round like peas, but rather slivers of butter with just enough volume to explode when they bake. (You'll be able to see the butter pieces even after adding the rest of the ingredients...so they aren't real small.) Toss the mixture as you mush around so that the end result is an even distribution of butter and flour throughout.

Pour the two cups of cold heavy cream into the flour mix all at once and stir to distribute and somewhat mix. You'll still be able to see dry flour around. Now, using your hands, knead the dough minimally to form a moveable ball.

Dust the counter surface with flour, dump the rough ball of dough and knead a couple more times just to have it hold together.

With a rolling pin, roll the dough with back and forth motions from center out - into a rectangle that is about 1 1/4" thick. Use the bench scraper to cut vertical lines about 3 inches wide. Now cut horizontal lines 3 inches apart. Use the bench scraper to remove the biscuits from the counter to a wax paper lined pan or cookie sheet. You can double stack the biscuits as long as you layer wax paper between. Use the partial squares to gently knead together to roll another smaller rectangle and make more biscuits.

FREEZE the biscuits fully—essential for success. The freezing is not optional. Bake as few or many as you need. Place them FROZEN on a cookie sheet lined with parchment...425 degree oven...22 minutes. You'll be amazed at the results.

*do not overmix

*bake straight from freezer to oven so that the butter-liquids will boil/explode and lift the biscuits!

*alter the size to suit your needs—and reduce or increase bake time

Biscuits—*quick and easy!*

Ever wish you had a really quick, fresh biscuit recipe either for breakfast or dinner...a recipe even kiddos can make? This is it—not as refined as the full scale biscuits, but certainly a delicious biscuit that you can drop on a cookie sheet and pop in the oven. I also use these in my dressing at Thanksgiving.

PREHEAT OVEN TO 475 DEGREES

One baking sheet with parchment
4 c flour • 2 T baking powder
2 t salt • 1 1/3 c whole milk • 2/3 c oil

Mix dry ingredients with a whisk to thoroughly blend. Do not short cut.

Add the liquids all at once and stir slightly immediately. Remember that you'll be trying to reduce gluten formation so don't over mix. You'll still see some degree of unincorporated flour.

OPTION 1: using your hands or a large spoon, portion out dough in the size biscuit you want and drop on cookie sheet leaving space around each.

Bake for about 10 - 13 minutes pending the size of your biscuits.

OPTION 2: dump dough on floured counter and knead a couple of times. Flatten out or use a rolling pin to 1" or 1.5" thickness and cut either in squares or use a round biscuit cutter. You can combine the left-over dough from cutting rounds to make more biscuits. Do not freeze these. Bake immediately about 10 - 13 minutes pending the size of your biscuits.

Serve these warm—with plenty of butter and jam!

This recipe doubles easily...but the dough does not freeze well.

Breakfast Bar

Your first bite will explain why this recipe is included. The bonus is that it is also gluten free. The WOW of the flavor makes this a recipe essential. You can cut these and wrap individually for the refrigerator or freezer—though they rarely make it there before they are gobbled up.

9 X 13 PAN WITH PARCHMENT
350 DEGREES PREHEATED
(16 BARS)

2 2/3 c oats
3/4 c sugar
3/4 c oat flour (or process / grind oats into "flour")
3/4 t salt
3/4 t Vietnamese cinnamon
3 c dried fruit & nuts (raisins or cranberries / pecans or walnuts)
1/2 c smooth peanut butter

1 1/2 t high quality vanilla
1/2 c melted butter
1/3 c maple syrup
(real maple or pancake syrup)
3 T corn syrup
1 1/2 T water

Mix dry ingredients (first 6) together.

Slightly warm together the peanut butter, maple & corn syrups in a glass measuring cup (microwave). Add the remaining wet ingredients together in a large bowl with this warm mix and stir well.

Stir the wet into the dry ingredients.

Press mixture into 9 x 13. A glove helps to keep it from sticking to your hand. Bake 32 min—until beginning to brown.

Cool, cut in half length-wise...then into 8 per side or whatever shape you'd like.

Breakfast Cookie

I wanted to provide a cookie that parents could get for their kiddos that would be healthy and delicious as a breakfast treat. When we tested this before opening the bakery, kiddos didn't like them—but parents loved them. Go figure! I almost cancelled this adventure but sold lots of these to adults.

PREHEATED 350 DEGREE OVEN

1/2 c mashed bananas (1 large) • 1/2 c peanut butter
1/2 c honey
2 t high quality vanilla • 1 c rolled oats
1/4 c wheat flour • 1/4 c milk powder
2 t Vietnamese cinnamon • 1 t baking soda
1/2 c cranberries or raisins
1/2 c sunflower seeds (raw or roasted)

In a large bowl mix the mashed banana, peanut butter, honey and vanilla. In a smaller bowl mix oats, flour, milk powder, cinnamon and soda.

Combine ingredients of both bowls together and add raisins (cranberries) and sunflower seeds. If too thick, add 2 T water.

Use a 1/4 c measuring cup per cookie dough—placed 3 inches apart on cookie sheet with parchment. Flatten using your hand/fingers to 2 3/4" rounds—1/2" thick.

Bake 15 - 17 minutes until slightly brown.

Store 3 days at room temp—or freeze for up to 2 months.

Breakfast Pie

How do you solve having a unique breakfast option that isn't sweet in a bakery? This is a terrific option that can be served immediately or made ahead and reheated. This is not a quiche—it is dense and hearty.

EACH PIE SERVES 7 - 8 SLICES

350 PREHEATED OVEN

PARTIALLY PRE-BAKED PIE SHELL - 10 AND 10
10 MINUTES WITH DRIED BEANS AND 10 WITHOUT

1 t salt
1/4 t pepper
dash nutmeg (about 1/8 t)
1 T sugar
1 T flour
1/2 can 4 oz green chilis drained
2 heaping T chopped onions cooked
3/4 c whole milk (1/2 c milk + 1/4 c half 'n half preferred)

3 eggs
2 c hash browns cooked/browned
(10 min. on parchment in oven)
Grated cheddar cheese—
about a cup
7 slices of cooked bacon torn
into pieces or
1 c precooked sausage crumbles

In a bowl, combine salt, pepper, nutmeg, sugar, flour, green chilis & onions. Add the milk and whisk—then the eggs and whisk again.

Line the bottom of the pie shell with cooked potatoes, top with bacon or sausage. Layer cheddar—not so much that the flavor overpowers the potatoes and meat. Pour the liquid mix over and top with slight sprinkling of cheese.

Bake 43 min.

VARIATIONS: Use any cooked meat you prefer or no meat at all. I do not like greasy meats, so I cook the bacon or sausage again for 4 minutes on parchment with paper towels layered over parchment and then spread the meat out. I also enjoy this pie with sautéed squash and red bell peppers instead of meat. Be creative!

Cinnamon Rolls

We always sold out of these long before lunch time.
The real key to this is the quality of the cinnamon and the butter.
This is not the initial recipe when I opened Lula Jane's—but rather the
third iteration in my ever constant attempt to have good—better—best!

OVEN 350

MAKES 16 LARGE OR MORE IF SMALLER

1 T + 1 t instant yeast
2/3 c sugar
6 c flour—all purpose
1 1/2 c wheat flour
2 t salt
1 c water—slightly warm
1 c milk—slightly warm
2 farm eggs
1 1/3 stick butter—very soft

You can use a stand mixer with a dough hook or mix/knead by hand if you are diligent and strong!

Put the dry ingredients into your mixing bowl and whisk really well.

-Knead for 15 minutes on medium speed. Check about halfway through to make sure that the flour at the bottom is incorporated for the remainder of the kneading process. If not, remove the bowl and turn the dough over and over in the bowl using your hands to get the flour totally involved and finish kneading.

Remove the dough hook, spray the mixer bowl with oil and cover the bowl with plastic wrap. Let rise til at least double. This varies depending on the humidity and the temperature of the room. You may need to be patient for 3 hours! I have been known to let this dough rise in a closed oven with the oven light on for heat.

Form into sweet rolls.

FILL:
1 c. melted butter; 1 c sugar whisked with 4 T Vietnamese cinnamon

Turn the dough out on a floured surface and hand shape into 24" long roll of dough. Using a rolling pin, roll the dough out to 10" x 24" slab. Slather the dough with melted butter and spread the sugar and cinnamon mix on top. Roll up the dough keeping the "log" 24" in length. Use the bench scraper and cut the roll in half (and continue as written).

Use the bench scraper and cut the roll in half—and each half into 8. Lay the sweet rolls into a sprayed roasting pan. And slather with melted butter.

For immediate use, bake for 34 minutes. Slather with butter and drizzle with 1/4 c half n half + 1/4 c heavy cream + powdered sugar mixed to consistency.

To save for later, bake 24 min. Freeze—or wrap for next day. Thaw and bake 17 min. Slather with butter...use drizzle...serve!

Scones Cranberry Orange

I have always guarded this recipe and not shared...so here it is for you. This is the end result of taking a fried scone from a Zen bakery recipe to a heart healthy baked scone. Not an easy process of morphing, but worth it to keep my hubby healthy with great treats. It is also a much easier scone to make than typical. Just remember that scones are a form of biscuits...so don't be afraid to experiment with different additions. Have fun with this recipe.

6 cups flour
1 c whole wheat flour
2/3 c sugar
2 t baking soda
4 heaping t cream of tartar
1/2 t salt
1 c of dried cranberries
1 c vegetable oil
1 T pure orange extract
2 1/2 c buttermilk

BIG BOWL - whisk all dry ingredients really well to thoroughly mix. Add the cranberries and break them up with your hands so they are not in clumps. I do this step down in the flour mix and toss to distribute well.

Add the wet ingredients all at once. Using a large spoon, stir the mixture until mostly wet. Two important things to note: gluten begins when you start stirring the dry and liquid together—and cream of tartar begins working immediately.

Turn out the mostly mixed contents onto a lightly floured surface and knead briefly to have it stick together. Divide into 5 piles—and with your hands, form each into a smooth ball and press the top with an open palm. You want to make a flattened ball about 1 1/2 inches high from each pile of dough.

Using a bench scraper, cut each ball into 4 triangles (cut the ball in half and then half again).

Place on parchment covered cookie sheets with space around each for rising and spreading.

BAKE IMMEDIATELY IN PRE HEATED OVEN:
    425 for 8 minutes
    Turn oven down to 350 and continue baking 4 minutes.

Serve with jam OR make a drizzle to pour over the top of each baked scone:

    1/2 c heavy cream
    1/2 c half and half
    1/2 t vanilla
    Powdered sugar to desired consistency

Scones

Use the biscuit recipe and add to ingredients list: 1 1/2 c cheese grated (cheddar, Swiss, parmesan, etc)

1 c chopped cooked small ham cubes
13 slices of cooked bacon
1 c pimientos drained (+ cheddar)

After pressing in the butter, toss in the meat and/or cheese of choice til well-distributed. I use my hands to do this so that the mix remains loose.

Add the 2 c of heavy cream and stir together. You may need another 1/4 to 1/2 c heavy cream with the increase in ingredients. Use just enough liquid to help the ingredients stick slightly together.

Knead a few times by hand to encourage the bind. Turn out on floured surface and knead a couple more times and form into a ball about 8" round. Using the bench scraper, cut the ball into two equal halves. Shape each half into a ball about 6 " wide and 2" high (sides straight up and not rounded). Again use the bench scraper to cut each ball in half and each half into 4 pie shaped scones. You will have 16 scones to place on wax paper and freeze.

The next day I pack the hard frozen scones into gallon zip lock bags and place back into the freezer. You can bake just one...or all in the future.

Bake FROZEN at 425 degrees for 22 minutes on parchment lined cookie sheet.

Dorothy's Zucchini Bread

1 LOAF

Dorothy was my mother-in-law and was famous for her zucchini bread. When she died early of cancer, her recipe was lost and the family was in a panic. After some searching, my daughter found the recipe on a card in Dorothy's handwriting—and everyone celebrated. This one was the biggest seller among breakfast breads at the bakery—hands down.

350 OVEN

stir together—no mixer needed
one loaf pan sprayed and floured
3 eggs
3/4 c oil
1 1/2 c sugar
1/3 c sour cream or buttermilk
3/4 t vanilla
3/4 t salt
3/4 t soda
3/4 t cinnamon
2 1/4 c flour
1 zucchini grated
3/4 c chopped nuts (pecans or walnuts)

No mixer needed! In large bowl, mix first 8 ingredients well with a whisk. Add the flour and mix well. Using a large spoon, stir in nuts and zucchini.

Spread in the prepared loaf pan. Bake 1 hr and 20 minutes.

This is a real show stopper!

Lunch & Dinner

Hummus

This makes a great lunch treat with tortilla chips, or a special treat for snacking. It is also very healthy and vegan/vegetarian. It may seem odd to make it with black beans or black-eyed peas—but oh my—so delicious. You'll never buy traditional hummus again. I enjoy this version of hummus because it doesn't have the "bite" of tahini.

And how easy is it using cans of beans & peas—though you can cook dried beans instead for this recipe.

> 2 cans chickpeas drained & rinsed
> 2 cans beans (black beans—blackeyes, etc)
> drained & rinsed
> 4 cloves garlic
> 1/3 to 1/2 c olive oil
> 1/4 c lemon juice
> 4 t cumin
> 2 T dried parsley or 1/3 c fresh chopped
> salt & pepper

Using a food processor mix all til smooth and serve with tortilla chips or crackers. Is that easy??? Store covered in the refrigerator for a week—if it lasts that long. I sometimes spread it in quesadillas or add it to tacos. Be creative.

Pimiento Cheese

This pimiento cheese was always a sell-out and is undoubtedly the best pimiento cheese I've ever had. If you think you aren't a pimiento cheese person, try this first. Don't feel intimidated about fresh mayo, use store-bought real mayo instead. And feel free to experiment with additional cheese options—like adding a bit of shredded parmesan.

Mayonnaise: (or use a high quality jar of mayonnaise)
1 egg
2 yolks
Squeeze of lemon • 1 T mustard
1 big cloves garlic • 1/4 t paprika
1/4 t cayenne
3/4 c light olive oil • 1/4 cup canola oil

In food processor, blend eggs, lemon, mustard, and garlic. After blended, slowly drizzle in oil. Blend until nice and thick. Add spices and mix.

1/2 large block white cheddar grated 1 cup feta crumbled

Mild to sharp grated cheddar (your preference) to taste 1 lg can pimiento drained, rinsed, and squeezed dry

1 bunch green onion sliced thin with some green included

Stir together white cheddar, feta, pimientos, green onion and mayonnaise. Then add yellow cheddar until you reach the right consistency. Not too wet (don't overdo the mayo).

This is a great recipe to adapt to your taste preference: quantity of pimientos, amount of mayo (though best if not too much), and amounts of cheeses. Make it like you prefer.

Potato-Corn Chowder
(serves a crowd!)

Is there a chill in the air? Need something delicious and hearty? This is also a flexible meal as you can add cooked chicken, shrimp, or fish. This draws you in and fills you up. Serve with tortilla chips, cornbread, or fresh slices of french bread.

5 lbs of potatoes (cubed and boiled with lots of salt) peeled or not
4 c corn (fresh or frozen)
6 whole garlic cloves (foil wrapped and baked 15 min at 350)
1 lg yellow onion diced
1 or 2 jalapeños diced (seeds removed)
2 red bell peppers diced
2 green bell peppers diced
2 quarts stock (vegetable or chicken)
5 c half-and-half warmed (microwave)
5 c whole milk—warmed • salt / pepper to taste
cayenne to taste (start with 1/4 t) • 2 T Worcestershire sauce

While potatoes are boiling, sauté the corn in a skillet over medium-high with about a tablespoon of oil. Stir and let them sizzle enough to brown.

Remove from heat and reserve.

In a large stock or soup pot, saute onion, jalapeños, chopped garlic, both chopped bell peppers for about 5 minutes until all are softened. The smell will be fabulous!

Add the stock until it just comes to a boil. Reduce the heat and stir in the warmed half and half—and the warmed milk. Add the potatoes (you can mash about 1/3 or them before adding to help thicken the chowder if you prefer), and the roasted corn. Stir well while it all warms together. Add the salt, pepper, cayenne, and Worcestershire sauce and adjust for taste.

Don't boil this chowder—just serve it quite warm.

Power Bowl

This is a flexible, variable main course meal that can be vegan, vegetarian, or with meat. All parts can be made ahead and refrigerated for a couple of days—then warmed and layered at serving time. Or use leftovers as components in the bowl. You can also make extra and freeze those pre-cooked ingredients for other dishes like tacos, etc.

Rice—either white or brown • Beans of choice—dried or canned
Corn—frozen or fresh kernels • Raw spinach
Onions • Cheese
Sauce: salsa, come back, guacamole, salad dressing…your choice Meat?

Rice cooked as directed on the package or use chicken or beef broth as the liquid, and/or spices of your choice (such as smoky paprika, cilantro, cumin, etc.).

BEANS: pinto, black beans, navy beans, red beans, black-eyed peas—choose one. You can boil dried beans or used canned beans rinsed and drained. Salt and pepper these to taste—and you can add picante or salsa to these for more flavor.

CORN: fresh or frozen corn—heat a skillet (medium high) so that you can brown the corn. Any oil + salt, pepper and paprika. Stir consistently watching for the browning magic to happen. This helps bring out the flavor.

<u>Raw spinach</u>—washed and torn or chopped.

CARAMELIZED YELLOW OR RAW CHOPPED PURPLE ONIONS: slice and half the yellow onions and slowly cook on low heat. This is an exercise in patience as they should be clear and sweet rather than brown and toasty.

STACKING AN INDIVIDUAL POWER BOWL:
THE ACTUAL QUANTITY IS BASED ON APPETITE

3/4 c cooked rice • 3/4 c cooked beans • 3/4 c browned corn
thin layer of caramelized onion • raw spinach, amount of choice
sprinkling of cheese: feta, mozzarella, cheddar or whatever
top individual bowl with sauce of choice or guacamole
(or make it super easy and top with a salad dressing or salsa)

Be creative with this and use the combination of ingredients of choice. You can also add pulled pork, chicken, shrimp, etc. above or below the bean layer.

Quesadillas

I enjoy making these as an easy lunch or dinner option that can be personalized per person. Just think ahead so you can roast the veggies you want to use: cauliflower, butternut squash, broccoli, mushrooms, etc. You can also include fresh spinach, tomatoes, avocado etc. Also prepare one of the sauces (or one you prefer) to serve with the quesadillas.

You will be folding the large burrito tortilla in half so your veggies, etc. cover just a half of the burrito.

Roast the veggies in oven after tossing lightly in olive oil, spreading on a parchment lined cookie sheet, and sprinkling with salt, pepper, paprika (or smoky paprika), or garlic salt—or any taste you are going for.

SUPPLIES / INGREDIENTS:

Large burrito flour tortillas (one per person)
Olive or vegetable oil for brushing before cooking
Cheese: cheddar, provolone, mozarella, parmesan
Roasted veggies or Fresh veggies

LAYERING THE QUESADILLA:

Fold the tortilla and crease slightly so you can define the half line. Now layer your chosen cheese, roasted and or raw veggies, more cheese. Fold the tortilla over the fill.

Heat a large sauté pan or griddle on medium. Brush the pan/griddle with olive oil or vegetable oil and do the same for one side of the quesadilla and place that side down on the hot pan to melt and lightly brown. Brush the other side with the oil and then flip the quesadilla to brown on the other side. I make it easy on myself and roll it over on the fold so that the contents don't spill out.

Done...except for the sauce that you should drizzle over the quesadilla or a puddle on the plate for dipping.

Quiche

Extraordinary…always a sell out. In fact, some will buy the cookbook just to get this recipe! We had quiche every Friday for lunch and just varied the ingredients weekly. This is the perfect recipe for experimenting: different cheeses, different roasted veggies. So many possibilities!

PREHEAT OVEN TO 350 DEGREES

EACH PIE SERVES 6 SLICES

ONE PIE	TWO PIES
1 partially baked pie shell	2 partially baked pie shells

FILL:

ONE PIE	TWO PIES
4 large eggs	8 large eggs
1/2 c heavy cream	1 c heavy cream
1 c whole milk	2 c whole milk
2 T ricotta cheese	4 T ricotta cheese
1/4 t kosher salt	1/2 t kosher salt
1 1/2 c roasted veggies	3 c roasted veggies
chopped herbs	chopped herbs
1 c cheese of choice	2 c cheese of choice

Bake the crust and set aside. This keeps the crust from becoming mushy when filled and baked.

Spread the roasted veggies on the bottom of the crust, sprinkle with herbs (fresh is preferable) and top with the shredded cheese(s).

Fill: warm the milk and cream together in microwave. In a bowl mix the milk/cream, ricotta, salt & eggs with an immersion blender. Try not to make it frothy - just well mixed.

Pour the liquid fill on top of the veggie-cheese in the pie crust.

If you have extra fill, save it in the refrigerator and add more eggs for scrambled eggs or an omelet the next morning!

Bake for 55 min. to 1 hr 10 min depending on oven and how full the crust is.

ROASTING VEGGIES:

Cut veggies, toss in a bowl with a bit of olive oil & salt/pepper.
Spread on parchment-lined baking sheet.
Bake at 350 for 15 to 30 minutes depending on type of vegetable.

POSSIBLE COMBINATIONS:

- tomato, basil, & mozzarella brussel sprouts & cheddar

- zucchini & mozzarella or cheddar + parmesan &
spread a little mustard on bottom of crust before filling

- butternut squash, sage & mozzarella or gouda caramelized onions, bacon & Swiss asparagus & parmesan & feta

- colorful bell peppers & gouda

Tomato Pie

Prepare to have a "life changing" experience when you eat tomato pie. Folks are always curious to know if this is like a quiche. NO! It is actually multiple layers of sliced fresh, juicy, flavorful tomatoes hand picked for perfect tomato examples. OH...TOMATO PIE! We could easily sell all of the slices of tomato pie within 45 minutes of beginning lunch service. So give this a try in the middle of summer when tomatoes are at their prime.

PREHEAT OVEN 350

MAKES 6 LARGE SERVING SLICES DIJON MUSTARD

2 1/4 lbs tomatoes thinly sliced
1 1/4 t salt, divided
1 sweet onion chopped
1 1/4 t freshly ground pepper, divided • 1 T oil
1/2 c assorted chopped fresh herbs (chives, parsley, basil, etc)
1/2 c grated Swiss cheese
1/2 c shredded parmesan • 1/3 c real mayo

Partially bake the pie crust (10 min. with beans/weights + 10 minutes without).

Layer the tomato slices sprinkled with salt between layers of paper towel and let sit for about 10 minutes to reduce the water.

While tomatoes are sitting, sauté onion & 1/4 t salt and pepper over medium heat about 3 minutes.

Smear thin layer of dijon mustard on bottom of crust and layer tomatoes, onion and herbs in the pie plate seasoning each layer with pepper. Layer until all the tomatoes are used.

Stir together the cheese and mayonnaise and spread over the pie. Bake for 30 min. until lightly browned.

Sweets

Blueberry Pie

A personal favorite—unleash this with your toughest critic and you'll still have a winner on your hands. The recipe has very little sugar so that the blueberries shine.

OVEN 350

ONE UNBAKED PIE SHELL &
DOUGH FOR TOP PIE CRUST

1/4 c + 2 T sugar
1/3 c + 2 T flour
3/4 t Vietnamese cinnamon
1/4 t salt
4 + c blueberries (fresh or frozen)
1 T fresh lemon juice
1 T melted butter
1 egg beaten

Whisk together sugar, flour, cinnamon and salt. In a larger bowl, measure the blueberries and toss in the dry mix to thoroughly coat the blueberries.

Pour the above blueberry mix into the unbaked pie shell. Drizzle with lemon juice and melted butter.

Top with pie crust, seal edges, and slit in several places for steam to escape.

Brush the top pie crust with beaten egg. Not required but does make the crust brown and shine.

Bake pie for 1 hour 15 minutes or until bubbling.

Cool for about an hour and a half before serving.

Bread Pudding

Surprise, surprise...the secret is the day old sweet rolls. It is a real game changer. So make sweet rolls for breakfast and save the leftovers for this recipe (that is, if you have leftovers).

350 OVEN

SPRAYED 9 X 13 PAN

7 sweet rolls cubed (day old is best)
1 c sugar
6 large eggs
3 c milk warmed
2 t vanilla

TOPPING:

1 c packed brown sugar
1/4 c (1/2 stick) butter softened
1 c chopped pecans or other nuts

SAUCE:

2 c sugar
1 c melted butter
2 eggs
4 t vanilla
1/2 c bourbon

Spread cubed sweet rolls in the pan. Mix together sugar, eggs, warm milk, and vanilla and pour evenly over the sweet roll cubes.

Let this sit about 30 minutes (or longer) so the bread becomes soggy.

With a fork, stir the topping together and crumble on top of bread pudding. Bake 30 minutes.

Sauce: While baking, put the sugar, melted butter and eggs into a heavy saucepan, whisk til well mixed, and bring to a gentle boil over medium heat. Once it reaches a rolling boil, remove from heat and set aside to cool slightly and add the vanilla and bourbon.

Cut the bread pudding into 12 servings, plate, and pour the sauce over individual servings.

Store the left over sauce in a large mason jar in the frig. (It is also great over ice cream, etc.)

Brownies

WOW...everyone loves these brownies.
And talk about super easy...winner / winner!
Make both pans and freeze one.

PREHEAT OVEN 350 DEGREES

ONE 9 X 13 PAN	TWO 9 X 13 PANS
4 oz unsweetened chocolate	8 oz unsweetened chocolate
3/4 c unsalted butter	1 1/2 c unsalted butter
4 large eggs	8 large eggs
2 c sugar	4 c sugar
1 1/3 c all purpose flour	2 2/3 c all purpose flour
3/4 t salt	1 1/2 t salt
1 t baking powder	2 t baking powder
2 t vanilla	1 T + 1 t vanilla
1 c semi-sweet chocolate chips	2 c semi-sweet chocolate chips

Spray pan(s) well.

Melt butter and unsweetened chocolate together (microwave) and set aside for next step.

In a stand mixing bowl or by hand, measure and add all ingredients except chocolate chips.

Attach the paddle and gently mix—turn off the mixer and stir by hand with a spatula to include the stuff sitting in the bottom of the bowl and around the sides. Use the mixer and paddle or spatula to completely incorporate all ingredients. DO NOT OVER MIX. You do not want to use high speed as the goal is not to incorporate air or to whip it. Stir in chocolate chips being sure to stir all the way to the bottom as well as the sides and immediately pour /spread into pan(s).

Bake 26 minutes.

Cool completely in the pan before cutting and/or frosting. Frosting ideas: chocolate, espresso, mint.

Buttermilk (Chess) Pie

Folks often ask what this tastes like, and my response is always "comfort food on steroids." It is truly a southern pie and was one of our two top selling pies and remarkably easy to make. Pay particular attention to the quality of your butter and vanilla! Eggs should be room temperature—always! Use real buttermilk and do not substitute.

PREHEAT OVEN 350 DEGREES

ONE PIE	TWO PIES
1 unbaked pie shell	2 unbaked pie shells
3 large eggs	6 large eggs
1 3/4 c sugar	3 1/2 c sugar
1/4 c all purpose flour	1/2 c all purpose flour
1/2 t salt	1 t salt
1/2 c warm buttermilk	1 c warm buttermilk
1/2 c melted butter	1 c melted butter
1 1/2 t vanilla extract	1 T vanilla extract

Melt the butter in a glass measuring cup in the microwave and add the buttermilk for an additional 20 seconds. The mixture should feel warm to the touch.

In a stand mixing bowl: measure and add all ingredients. Attach the paddle and gently mix—turn off the mixer and stir by hand with a spatula to include the stuff sitting in the bottom of the bowl and on the sides—use the mixer and paddle again to completely incorporate all ingredients. You do not want to use high speed as the goal is not to incorporate air or to whip it. Stir again and pour all liquid into pie shell(s) and bake on baking sheet 1 hr 10 min.

By hand with no mixer: measure and add all ingredients to a mixing bowl. Stir with a whisk, spatula, or spoon to thoroughly stir / mix the ingredients.

do not whip or add air. Pour into pie shell(s) and bake on a baking sheet in the oven for 1 hr 10 min.

If it has a grainy texture after baking, you have not given enough time in mixing for the sugar to be completely incorporated. Next time mix / stir a little longer.

Buttermilk Pound Cake

This recipe requires not only great butter, vanilla and buttermilk, but also requires full attention to the process of mixing. I had a 30% failure rate when I began working on this recipe, but now have a 100% success rate!

PREHEAT OVEN 350 DEGREES

One Cake Bundt pan with crisco and flour
1 c high quality butter at room temp
3 c sugar
1 t pure almond extract
1 1/4 t pure vanilla extract
4 large eggs
3 c all purpose flour
1/4 t salt
1/4 t baking soda
1 c warm buttermilk

In a stand mixing bowl with paddle, beat the butter and sugar until fully creamed—the color of cream—about 10 minutes on medium. Do not skimp on creaming time. as this encourages the "melting" of the sugar into the butter so the cake is not "grainy." Add the almond and vanilla and mix thoroughly.

While the butter and sugar are creaming, mix the dry ingredients in a separate bowl.

Prepare the bundt pan by coating with Crisco—do not miss any spots! Using 1/4 c of flour, shake the pan so that it is covered with the flour and dump out the extra by knocking the pan upside down on the edge of the trash can.

Add the eggs one at a time to the butter/sugar/extract mix. Stop the mixer and stir with a spatula to incorporate ingredients on the bottom and sides of the bowl.

From here on, take care not to over-mix as it will increase the formation of gluten forming and the pound cake will be tough. (Yuck)

Using the mixer, add the flour and buttermilk by alternating each and hand mixing at points noted. Do NOT skip the hand mixing—a real key to success.

Add a cup of dry mix and lightly mix. Add 1/2 cup of buttermilk and lightly mix. Add one more cup of dry mix and lightly mix. Using a spatula, wipe off some of the batter from the spatula, remove the bowl, and hand stir the batter by going all the way to the bottom of the bowl and folding over and into the remaining batter. Do this several times.

Replace the bowl and add the last of the buttermilk, mix lightly. Add the remaining dry mix and mix lightly. Now again use the spatula and remove batter from the paddle, remove the bowl, and repeat the hand mixing scraping bottom and sides of bowl to incorporate all ingredients until smooth.

The hand mixing insures that the areas the paddle cannot reach actually are incorporated into the full batter. Paddles cannot scrape the bowl completely—so you must do this. This is one of the keys to success.

Pour this into the bundt pan using the spatula to do a last stir around at the top. Bake for 1 hour 15 minutes.

Remove from oven and let sit 15 to 20 minutes. Timing is everything in having it come out of the pan perfectly. "Bang" the bundt pan bottom down on the counter to loosen slightly. Now turn it over as you "bang" the bundt pan upside down on wax paper on the counter. The pound cake should come out perfectly!

Carrot Cake

Carrot cake comes in all kinds of versions. This version is so moist, with tall layers—looks regal when frosted with either cream cheese frosting or white frosting. Never a disappointment. You can grate the carrots by hand or use a food processor.

OVEN 350

2 LAYER 8"	2 LAYER 9"
3 c shredded carrots	4 c shredded carrots
2 c sugar	3 c sugar
1 1/4 c oil	1 3/4 c oil
1 t salt	1 1/2 t salt
3 c flour	4 1/2 c flour
1 t baking soda	1 1/2 t baking soda
2 t baking powder	1 T baking powder
2 t cinnamon	1 T cinnamon
4 eggs	6 eggs
1 c raisins	1 1/2 c raisins
1 c chopped pecans	1 1/2 c chopped pecans

In the mixer with a paddle, beat oil, salt and sugar til well blended. Combine flour, cinnamon, baking powder, and soda in a bowl. Add this to the creamed mix alternately with eggs. Scrape the bottom and sides of the mixing bowl and mix well.

Stir in carrots and optional raisins and/or nuts.

Pour in pans prepped with an oil spray and parchment circles.

Bake for about 55 minutes or until the center of each layer offers some resistance when pressed in the middle.

Cool, turn out, and freeze before frosting.

Cherry Pie

This is a winner-winner with the nutmeg and cinnamon. If you use frozen cherries, thaw and drain the cherries overnight by putting them in a colander and large bowl in the refrigerator. Save the juice to use later as liquid in a simple syrup to serve over pancakes. I never waste anything!

ONE 9" PIE

PREHEAT OVEN 425 THEN LOWER TO 375

4 1/2 c cherries halved (mix of tart and sweet)
1/2 c + 2 T sugar
2 T lemon juice
3 T cornstarch pinch nutmeg
1/4 t Vietnamese cinnamon
Double crust for pie

If you use frozen cherries, be sure to thaw and drain thoroughly. I try to drain overnight in a colander sitting in a bowl in the refrigerator. Mix cherries, 1/2 c sugar & lemon juice. Set aside for 5 min.

Mix remaining sugar, cornstarch, nutmeg and cinnamon. Add this mix to the cherry mix—and pour into pie shell. Cover top of pie with 3/4 inch strips of crust, lattice style. or a solid top crust with slits to release the steam.

Brush with heavy cream or a beaten egg. Sprinkle sugar on top. Bake 15 min at 450...and reduce to 375 for another 35 - 40 min.

Serve with vanilla ice cream...or let the pie stand on its own! Step back and enjoy the compliments.

Chocolate Chip Cookies

Amongst our customers, these cookies have a loyal following.
They declare that there are none to compare.
Do not cut corners or short cut time as everything plays a roll in the
perfection. Great ingredients and a particular process are the keys.
It really does involve several days to get the very best product—so plan
ahead. Be sure to have a scale that will measure in ounces and grams
if possible. All ingredients must be at room temperature.

HINT: before you launch into the recipe, you might want to brown the butter. And while the butter is browning, you can measure and thoroughly mix the dry ingredients...oh so organized.

OVEN 350

PARCHMENT LINED PAN MAKES 23 - 75 G COOKIES OR
30 - 60 G COOKIES

2 c minus 2 T cake flour
1 2/3 c bread flour
1 1/4 t baking soda
1 1/2 t baking powder
1 1/2 t coarse salt—kosher
8 oz (2 sticks) unsalted butter (browned to make
7 oz) 5 oz (1 1/4 sticks) unsalted butter softened
1 1/4 c light brown sugar
1 c + 2 T granulated sugar
2 lg eggs
2 t vanilla
12 oz dark chocolate chips (just under 2 c)
4 oz milk chocolate chips (just under 2/3 c)

BROWNED BUTTER: use a heavy saucepan—melt 8 oz of butter (1 cup) and then simmer / low boil for 20 to 30 minutes on medium low heat. Be patient - do not rush this as you will burn the butter and have to start over. The butter will eventually begin turning amber and smell marvelous.

Let it cool to room temp — even setting in the refrigerator if you want to use it right away. This process will leave you with about 7 oz of browned butter (because the water in the butter has boiled off).

While the butter is browning, whisk together flours, baking soda, baking powder, & salt really well in a bowl and set aside.

In a stand mixer with paddle attachment cream the 5 oz of butter, browned butter, granulated and light brown sugars. Usually takes 5 - 10 minutes for the butters to help dissolve and incorporate the sugars. This mixture will look soft and slightly fluffy. Add the eggs one at a time, beating well after each addition. Now add the vanilla and mix well. It is fine to do lots of mixing up to this point. However, once you begin introducing the dry ingredients, keep the mixing to a minimum so that the cookies are not tough and rubbery.

Add the dry ingredients a cup at a time, stopping a couple of times to scrape the sides and bottom of the mixing bowl with a spatula. Before adding the chocolate chips, use the spatula to scrape and fold in the dough in the bottom of the bowl. This will help the cookies bake evenly. Add the chips and mix until evenly distributed in the dough.

Place in the refrigerator covered and chill batter 24 to 48 hours. This is part of the gluten forming process. Don't skip it.

•USING A SCALE, MEASURE INDIVIDUAL COOKIES

Line a cookie sheet with waxed paper and roll the dough into balls. Select a "size" in grams and weigh each portion of dough so they are equal.

75 g. for larger cookies
60 g. for regular size cookies

When you shape each cookie, just apply enough pressure to have the dough stick together in a general ball shape. These will be somewhat irregular, but do not roll them between your hands to make them into "pretty balls". This would over work your dough and that's a NO.

CHOCOLATE CHIP COOKIES

Freeze the balls overnight—you can then bake them or dump them into a zip lock freezer bag and store in the freezer for use.

Bake the cookie balls straight from the freezer on parchment paper:

> 75 g large size—20 minutes
> 60 g regular size—18 minutes

Let them cool on the cookie sheet if you can resist eating them hot! Be mindful that they'll not have as much crispy outside if you eat them hot.

When they are cool, they are crisp on the outside and chewy on the inside. OH MY!

Chocolate Cake (super moist)

This cake has been such a surprise. We began making it because it is vegan—and then customers began requesting it instead of our regular chocolate cake. They just love how moist it is. So it became the chocolate cake of choice. YUM

PREHEAT OVEN - 350 DEGREES

LIGHTLY SPRAY CAKE PANS AND LINE WITH PARCHMENT CIRCLES.

8" 2 LAYER	9" 2 LAYER
2 1/3 c flour	4 c flour
2 c brown sugar	3 c brown sugar
1/2 c cocoa	3/4 c cocoa
2 t soda	1 T soda
1 t salt	1 1/2 t salt
2 c water (warm)	3 c water (warm)
2/3 c canola or veggie oil	1 c canola or vegetable oil
2 t white vinegar	1 T white vinegar
1 t vanilla	1 1/2 t vanilla
1/2 c chocolate chips*	3/4 c chocolate chips*

Dump everything into the mixing bowl except chocolate chips and mix well (mixer or by hand). (Do not eliminate the vinegar as it plays a role in leavening.)

Add the chocolate chips, stir, pour into the cake pans.

*You ask—What kind of chocolate chips? You choose: semi sweet, milk, dark, mini, regular. It really doesn't matter—just have fun with it.

Bake:
  8" - about 35 minutes
  9" - about 40 minutes-

These cakes "mound" while baking so don't be surprised. You can slice the mound off the top when you frost—and this makes a delicious treat for yourself!

Also peel the parchment off very slowly and carefully as the chocolate chips will stick to it. You'll have to leave some on the paper, but most will be in the cake!

Coconut Cream Pie

This was such a difficult recipe for me to develop since
I'm not a big fan of coconut, so I asked folks what to include -
and then didn't like the taste of the outcome of their advice.
I decided coconut pie should taste like real coconut—not extracts
or additives! Here it is...one of our top selling pies!

ONE PIE	TWO PIES
9" pie crust	2 9" pie crusts
7 oz bag sweetened coconut	14 oz bag sweetened coconut
3 egg yolks	6 egg yolks
3/4 c sugar	1 1/2 c sugar
1/4 t salt	1/2 t salt
2 1/4 c whole milk	4 1/2 c whole milk
1/4 c corn starch	1/2 c corn starch
1 t vanilla	2 t vanilla
1 1/2 T butter	3 T butter
1/4 c powdered sugar	1/2 c powdered sugar
1 1/2 c heavy whipping cream	3 c heavy whipping cream

350 DEGREES: Bake the raw pie crust 14 minutes weighted with wax paper and dried beans (I use pinto). Then remove the beans and wax paper and bake 14 additional minutes. Let the crust cool on the counter while you make the cream fill.

Spread coconut on parchment-covered cookie sheet and bake 4 min. in preheated 350 oven. This brings out the flavor of the coconut without drying it out.

In a heavy bottom sauce pan, combine the egg yolks, sugar & salt. With a glass measuring cup, warm the whole milk (minus 1/2 c or 1 c pending one or two pies) in the microwave in order to acclimate the egg yolks before putting them on the stove. Add this portion of the milk and using a heavy whisk, stir this mixture. Use the whisk for stirring only—not for beating and actually whisking! Warm the remaining milk a bit more in the microwave and use the whisk to stir in the corn starch. Now add to the sauce pan mixture and stir again.

Over medium heat, exercise patience as you gently stir and cook the mixture. It will take about 7 minutes depending on the heat—and you will begin to see bubbles. Wait until the bubbles are like volcanoes—and stir gently for one more minute.

Remove from the heat and stir in the vanilla and butter. Switch to a rubber spatula and fold in the coconut, stirring until well incorporated. Pour into the pie crust(s) and chill in the refrigerator for a couple of hours or until just before serving.

With an electric mixer and whisk attachment, combine powdered sugar and heavy cream and whip until firm peaks form. You'll know because the mixture will almost begin turning yellow...but stop at that point or you will have butter! Pile the whipped cream on top of the pie using a spatula to form peaks and valleys. Chill til time to serve. YUM!

French Silk Pie

This is a chocolate mousse filled pie that is amazing. It only requires patience and very little talent or knowledge. It is so rich that you can serve more people with one pie than for the typical pie. It is just as easy to make 2 pies and freeze one for a later event or gift. It does require a pre-baked pie crust or a crushed Oreo crust (so easy). Do not use a graham cracker crust as it demeans the final product. With the fresh whipped cream on top, it is a show stopper.

ONE PIE	TWO PIES
1 c unsalted butter softened	2 c unsalted butter softened
1 1/2 c sugar	3 c sugar
1 1/2 t vanilla	1 T vanilla
1 t espresso powder	2 t espresso powder
4 oz melted unsweetened baker's chocolate (bar)	8 oz melted unsweetened baker's chocolate (bar)
4 lg eggs at room temp.	8 lg eggs at room temp

Using a stand mixer and paddle, cream the butter and sugar on a speed between low and medium for 5 minutes.

Turn off the mixer, scrape inside and bottom with spatula and add the vanilla and espresso powder. Continue beating for 5 more minutes.

Add the melted chocolate. (My microwave has a melt function and does a great job without ever burning the chocolate. If yours doesn't have this function, you can melt the chocolate over time using small shots of 20 seconds, checking after each 20 second interval, stirring, and cautiously continuing.) Continue beating for 5 minutes.

Add one egg at a time—beating 5 minutes after each addition. The key here is patience. Once all eggs have been beaten into the mousse for 5 minutes, turn the mixer off and stir and scrape really well. It is a good idea to taste the mouse to see if the sugar has mostly dissolved. If not, add another 5 minutes.

Using a spatula, pour the fill into the crust(s). Chill in the refrigerator for a couple of hours to set the fill.

Top the pie(s) with whipped cream. Pour 1 3/4 c heavy whipping cream per pie in a clean mixing bowl. Add 1/3 c powdered sugar per pie to the mixing bowl and stir with the whisk before attaching it to the mixer. This will prevent the powdered sugar from blowing around the mixer. Beginning with slow speed, turn the mixer on and gradually increase the speed to the maximum. I drape the mixer with a dish towel over the top of the mixer and bowl to keep it from splattering all around. You will want to keep an eye on the cream as it mixes—as you are watching for the color to change from white to almost yellow. Be very careful—if it makes it to yellow, you'll have butter. If you do not get close to yellow, the whipped cream won't stand up over time. Spread, lift and peak the whipped cream on the pie(s)—not trying to make a smooth topping. You can dress it up a bit more by grating some chocolate on top like snow—a nice professional touch.

Store in the refrigerator until serving time that day/evening or the next day. If you want to freeze it (them), do this before adding the whipped cream.

When you are planning to use it or give it, remove from the freezer and place in the refrigerator to thaw and add fresh whipped cream.

Keep in mind that this is made with raw eggs, so it must be either refrigerated or frozen all the time for food safety.

Enjoy!

Fudge Pie

This is a super easy, deep, dark, rich, gooey pie that can be made crustless, in a pie shell, or tart pan. Because it is so rich and slices easily, it can serve more people.

PREHEAT OVEN TO 350 DEGREES

ONE PIE	TWO PIES
1 unbaked pie shell	2 unbaked pie shells
or bake crustless	or no crusts at all
3 large eggs	6 large eggs
1 1/2 c sugar	3 c sugar
1/3 c all purpose flour	2/3 c all purpose flour
1/3 c dark special cocoa	2/3 c dark special cocoa
3/4 c melted butter	1 1/2 c melted butter
1 1/2 t vanilla extract	1 T vanilla extract

In a stand mixing bowl or by hand: measure and add all ingredients. Attach the paddle and gently mix—turn off the mixer and stir by hand with a spatula to include the stuff sitting in the bottom of the bowl—use the mixer and paddle or spatula or whisk to completely incorporate all ingredients.

You do not want to use high speed as the goal is not to incorporate air or to whip it. Pour all liquid into pie shell(s). If baking without crust, use a glass pie plate and gently spritz with oil spray. Bake on baking sheet about 38 minutes depending on how deep your pie contents are.

If it has a grainy texture, you have not given enough time in mixing for the sugar to be completely incorporated. Next time mix / stir a little longer.

You can also add other goodies before baking: pecans, chocolate chips, dried cherries, etc. Or pour caramel sauce over the top after baking. Have fun experimenting.

German's Chocolate Cake

So why the apostrophe? Most folks think that it is a cake originating in Germany. Instead it is made with a light chocolate developed by a baker named "German." Thus the accurate name for the cake is German's.

Surprise—surprise! I figure what people really like about this cake is the fill and topping that includes lots of options based on this recipe.

350 OVEN

PREPARE PANS WITH SPRAY AND PARCHMENT ROUNDS

2 LAYER 8"	2 LAYER 9"
4 eggs separated	6 eggs separated
4 oz german's chocolate	6 oz german's chocolate
1 c water	3/4 c water
1 c butter	1 1/2 c butter
2 c sugar	3 c sugar
1 t vanilla	1 1/2 t vanilla
2 1/2 c cake flour	3 3/4 c cake flour
1 t baking soda	1 1/2 t baking soda
1/2 t salt	1 t salt
1 c buttermilk	1 1/2 c buttermilk

Beat egg whites and save in a separate bowl for later.

In the egg white mixing bowl, cream the butter and sugar for 10 minutes while melting the chocolate.

After the creamed mix is light and fluffy, add the chocolate, vanilla and water.... mixing well.

In a separate bowl, mix the cake flour, soda and salt. Then alternately add this with warm buttermilk—always beginning and ending with the flour mix. Scrape and stir the bottom and side of the bowl.

GERMAN'S CHOCOLATE CAKE

Then using a spatula, fold in the egg whites til just incorporated. Pour the dough into the pans and bake for 38 (45 - 9") minutes.

Cool, remove from pans, lightly wrap in saran and freeze.

Use the chocolate frosting recipe for the entire cake with these addition choices: between layers: chopped pecans, coconut, caramel drizzle, ganache drizzle, mini chocolate chips on top: make choices from the above roster

A traditional German's chocolate cake has a specific icing—more complicated—and this gets rave reviews as well.

Italian Creme Cake

This is a dress-up cake, a specialty cake that shouts,
"I'm a terrific baker" when you serve this. I'm not a big coconut fan,
but it is essential in the overall execution of this cake—delicious.
Be sure to grind the nuts and coconut well using a food processor.

OVEN 350

2 LAYER 8" 2 LAYER 9"

Prep the cake pans with spray and parchment rounds. Separate the eggs saving the yolks in a small bowl or cup for later. In a mixer with whisk attachment, beat the egg whites to soft peaks so they remain moist.

Remove to a separate bowl for later.

5 eggs separated	8 eggs separated
1 c butter warm	1 1/2 c butter warm
2 c sugar	3 c sugar
1 t vanilla	1 1/2 t vanilla
2 c flour	3 c flour
1 t soda	1 1/2 t soda
1 c buttermilk warm	1 1/2 c buttermilk warm
1 c pecans chopped well	1 1/2 c pecans chopped well
1 c coconut (food processor)	1 1/2 c coconut (food processor)

Using the empty egg white bowl and a paddle cream the sugar, butter and vanilla for about 10 minutes until fluffy. Add egg yolks one at a time and beat well for each.

Set aside a separate bowl of flour and soda mixed well. Add the dry ingredients mix alternately starting with dry and alternating with buttermilk—ending with dry ingredients. Add pecans and coconut.

Remove the paddle and hand fold in the egg whites just until incorporated fairly well. Mixing too long will contribute to a tough, dry cake.

Pour into prepared pans and bake about 44 minutes. Test for resistance in the top of the middle of each layer.

Let cool slightly and then turn out for cooling and freezing layers for frosting.

Use either cream cheese or white frosting and sprinkle the top of the cake generously with chopped pecans.

Gorgeous and so delicious…an elegant cake.

Key Lime Pie

This pie is the real deal in key lime pies. However, without the customary food coloring, the pie fill looks yellow rather than green. But one bite will convince anyone that this is better than the recipes that try to fool you with green food coloring! Stick to the recipe.

PREHEAT OVEN 350

9" PIE SHELL PARTIALLY BAKED
(10 MIN. WITH BEANS + 10 WITHOUT)

FILLING:

6 large egg yolks
zest of one lime
1 1/2 cans (14 oz each) sweetened condensed milk
1/2 can evaporated milk
1 c key lime juice (like Nellie & Joe's—not regular lime juice)

Zest the lime.

Use electric mixer and paddle to beat together egg yolks and zest for about 1 minute.

Add both milks to mixing bowl and mix. Add lime juice last and mix for about a minute. You will notice the mixture thickening—this is because the lime juice "cooks" the yolks. Pour into the pie shell.

With pie on cookie sheet, bake for 17 minutes.

Cool and allow to set for 45 minutes. Refrigerate uncovered at least 1 more hour before serving.

This pie can be frozen—and covered once frozen.

Oatmeal Chocolate Chip Cookies

I raised my kiddos with these cookies—and most of the neighborhood kiddos as well. So my mixer was in use every day! I make them with unsalted butter. I tried making them with half butter and half browned butter to give more depth and flavor to the cookie. However, oats are not receptive to the flavors in brown butter. So no need to take the extra effort. The texture of these cookies is terrific.

MAKES ABOUT 17 COOKIES @ 85 GRAMS PER

PREHEAT OVEN 350

2 sticks butter
2 eggs
2 c brown sugar 1 t soda
1 1/2 t salt
2.5 t vanilla
2 heaping cups flour
2 cups long cook oats (not instant)
2 c chocolate chips

Cream first ingredients (butter, eggs, sugar) really well (about 10 minutes). Add, in order, remaining ingredients. Refrigerate a bit so that the dough isn't so sticky to weigh.

Measure 45 g. or 60 g, flatten slightly and freeze. Bake on parchment lined cookie sheet. Bake 17 min. from freezer.

45 g - 16 min. from freezer; 60 g - 17 min. from freezer

Oatmeal Raisin Cookies

These oatmeal raisins cookies have a fantastic texture for an oatmeal cookie. In fact, of all the cookies I make, my husband likes these the most. They are not gummy or crispy thin...just right!

MAKES ABOUT 20 75 G COOKIES

MAKES ABOUT 24 60 G COOKIES

PREHEAT OVEN 350

1 c butter
2 eggs
2 c brown sugar
1 t soda
1 1/4 t salt
2 1/2 t vanilla
2 rounded cups flour
1 t Asian cinnamon
2 cups long cook oats (not instant)
2 c raisins

Cream first ingredients (butter, eggs, brown sugar) really well (about 10 minutes). Add, in order, remaining ingredients.

Measure 75 g or 60 g and flatten somewhat by hand. These can be frozen and baked later—or baked right after making the dough. Bake on cookie sheet lined with parchment. Bake 18 minutes from freezer.

60 g - 17 min from freezer

75 g 18 min from freezer

Peanut Butter Crunch Pie

Rich beyond words—very much in demand—and cumbersome to make. Worth the effort if you love peanut butter and chocolate. The necessary peanut brittle recipe is at the end of this one.

Make the brittle first or the day ahead and store in zip lock bag forcing out as much air as possible.

CRUSHED OREO CRUST:

20 cookies crushed slightly
1/2 c melted butter

Mix the two above and spread and pat into 9" pie plate

Sprinkle some peanut brittle on top of the Oreo crust.

FILLING:

6 oz cream cheese at room temp
1 c creamy peanut butter
2 T vanilla
3/4 c dark brown sugar
1 1/2 c heavy cream at room temp

Using a mixer with paddle: blend cream cheese, peanut butter, vanilla & brown sugar til smooth & blended. Scrape sides and bottom of bowl and transfer to another bowl.

Using a whisk on the mixer, whip the heavy cream until fluffy and gently stir this into the peanut butter mix. Pour over the brittle in the pie plate and smooth the top. Sprinkle more crumbled peanut brittle on top.

TOPPING: (GANACHE)

3 oz dark chocolate chips
2 T butter at room temp
1 t light corn syrup
1/4 c heavy cream warmed

In the microwave, melt chocolate, butter & corn syrup. Heat cream until quite warm and pour over the above mixture. Let it sit for a minute to let the chocolate chips begin to melt. Using a whisk, stir until this becomes a smooth mixture. If it looks like grated chocolate in chocolate milk, just warm all of it in the microwave for 20 seconds or so and continue whisking until chocolatey smooth.

Drizzle this over the top of the pie. Finished! Store this pie in the refrigerator for several days.

PEANUT BRITTLE:

1/2 c sugar 2 T butter
1 T light corn syrup
2 T water

Put above ingredients in a heavy saucepan on medium high until it begins to brown. Reduce to medium letting it lightly boil until golden.

WHILE IT IS COOKING, HAVE A SMALL BOWL READY WITH:

1/4 t soda
3/4 t salt
1 1/2 c chopped peanuts
(choose either salted or unsalted but not dry roasted)

Be ready for the last step as you'll find the peanut brittle sets up really fast when you add the nut mixture.

Remove the amber/golden mix from the stove and add the peanut mixture. Stir and turn out on waxed paper to cool.

Crumble for use—and store the extra in an airtight bag to munch on or use in the near future—perhaps in brownies or in/on a cake, or some other dish.

Pecan Pie – Bourbon

I put this in as a two pie recipe because it is likely criminal to make only one when you can give one away or serve a larger crowd. However, if you prefer, just half the recipe and make only one pie. This makes a great Thanksgiving or Christmas present - such a treat. And this is an easy recipe. As an option, you can add some dark chocolate chips before pouring into the pie plate.

TWO UNBAKED CRUSTS

OVEN 350

FILLING: (THIS DOUBLE BATCH = 2 REGULAR PIES)

1 1/2 c sugar
2 1/2 c dark corn syrup
1/4 c bourbon
3 T butter melted
6 eggs
1 T vanilla
1 t salt
1 T flour
3.5 c large-chopped pecans baked for 4 minutes to enhance the flavor

Put the pecans in the pie shells first.

Combine in mixer sugar, dark corn syrup, salt, flour & eggs. Mix well. Stir in remaining ingredients. Pour into pie shells over the pecans.

Bake for 1 hr 12 min. Let rest 2 to 3 hours.

Pumpkin Pie With Streusel Topping

This recipe makes an amazing pumpkin pie because of the diversity of the spices. Some are unexpected and add a real depth of flavor to the pie.

ONE PIE SHELL—UNCOOKED

2 c (one can) pure pumpkin
1/2 14 oz can sweetened condensed milk
1/2 can or 7 oz evaporated milk
1/4 c brown sugar • 2 eggs
2 1/2 t cinnamon • 1/2 t salt
1/4 t cardamom • 1/4 t ginger

Mix all ingredients well and pour into pie shells. Bake 10 min. at 425—reduce heat & bake 375 for 25 min—add streusel topping and bake 10 min more.

STREUSEL TOPPING:

3/4 c pecans—toasted & chopped
1/4 c light brown sugar
2 T flour
2 t cinnamon
2 T butter

Mix brown sugar, flour & cinnamon. Add toasted pecans to coat well. Cut in cold butter with a fork. This should be chunky so that you can use your hand to break it up and sprinkle on the pie.

Can be stored in frig up to 4 days.
Or can be frozen.

You can also make the pie without the streusel topping.

Red Velvet Cake

Not sure why folks love Red Velvet Cake. To me, this is a glorified, barely chocolate, orange cake with lots of flavorless red food coloring! Go figure—but here is a great recipe for it.

350 OVEN

PREP PANS WITH SPRAY AND PARCHMENT CIRCLES.
2 LAYER 9"

2 c sugar
1 c butter—room temp • 3 eggs
1 1/2 t vanilla
1 1/2 T water
2 T red food coloring
1 T orange zest
2 1/2 t flour
2 t baking powder • 1/4 t soda
1/4 c cocoa
1 c warm buttermilk

Begin creaming sugar and butter until light and fluffy with a paddle on the mixer.

While creaming, use a separate bowl to mix flour, soda, baking powder and cocoa.

To the creamed mixture add the eggs one at a time, mixing after each egg. Add vanilla, water, food coloring, and zest—mixing well.

Alternate flour mixture and buttermilk to the mixer just until incorporated well.

Pour into prepared pans and bake about 38 minutes. Freeze the layers lightly wrapped before frosting with cream cheese frosting or white frosting.

Cake: White

It is so hard to make a white cake that stays moist—and
I have tried many recipes and adapted them
as well. This version really does work.

These layers will be nice and tall for a beautiful cake.
Add sprinkles at the last minute to the dough and you'll have
a confetti cake! If your cake layers fall you can most often
"blame" it on uneven mixing or lack of enough bake time.

8" 2 LAYER	9" 2 LAYER
1 c butter room temp	1 1/8 c butter room temp
2 c sugar	2 1/2 c sugar
3 c cake flour	3 3/4 c cake flour
2 1/4 t baking powder	1 T baking powder
3/8 t soda	3/4 t soda
1 1/4 t salt	1 1/2 t salt
6 egg whites (room temp)	7 egg whites (room temp)
2/3 c sour cream room temp	3/4 c sour cream room temp
1 1/2 t vanilla	2 t vanilla
1 1/2 t almond extract	2 t almond extract
1 1/4 c whole milk warm	1 1/2 c whole milk warm

Begin creaming the butter and sugar in a stand mixer with paddle—medium speed for 5 - 10 minutes.

While the mixer does the creaming work, measure all dry ingredients in a bowl, whisk to combine and set aside.

To the creamed mix, add the egg whites, then sour cream, vanilla and almond—scraping the sides and bottom of the mixing bowl to insure an even mixture.

Beginning and ending with the dry ingredients, add about a third of dry, then half the milk, etc. until all mixed in. Do NOT over mix—just until incorporated well. Use the spatula to again scrape sides and bottom of bowl and mix one last time.

Pour equal amounts into lightly sprayed pans with bottoms lined with parchment circles.

8" - bake 38 minutes
9" - bake 44 minutes

You can test by lightly pressing your finger on the center of the layer. If it doesn't have any resistance, add about 3 minutes baking time. If it isn't done, it will fall in the middle.

Wicked Pie

This is what it looks like when being creative with a recipe.
I wanted to offer something spectacular during the Christmas season,
so I amended the buttermilk pie recipe. It is still remarkably easy to make.

Pay particular attention to the quality of your butter and vanilla!
Eggs should be room temperature—always!
Use real buttermilk and do not substitute.

PREHEAT OVEN TO 350 DEGREES

ONE PIE	TWO PIES
1 unbaked pie shell	2 unbaked pie shells
3 large eggs	6 large eggs
1 3/4 c sugar	3 1/2 c sugar
1/4 c all purpose flour	1/2 c all purpose flour
1/2 t salt	1 t salt
1/2 c warm buttermilk	1 c warm buttermilk
1/2 c melted butter	1 c melted butter
1 1/2 t vanilla extract	1 T vanilla extract
1/2 apple chopped small	1 apple peeled/chopped small
1/2 c chopped pecans	1/2 c chopped pecans
1/2 c chocolate chips	1 c chocolate chips
1/3 c chopped dried cherries	2/3 c chopped dried cherries

In the bottom of the pie shell(s) spread the apple pieces, chopped pecans, chocolate chips and dried cherries. Set aside for later.

I melt the butter in a glass measuring cup in the microwave and add the buttermilk for an additional 20 seconds. The mixture should feel warm to the touch.

In a stand mixing bowl: measure and add all ingredients. Attach the paddle and gently mix—turn off the mixer and stir by hand with a spatula to include the stuff sitting in the bottom of the bowl and on the sides—use the mixer and paddle to completely incorporate all ingredients. You do not want to use high speed as the goal is not to incorporate air or to whip it.

Stir again and pour all liquid into pie shell(s) and bake on baking sheet 1 hr 10 min.

BY HAND WITH NO MIXER: measure and add all ingredients to a mixing bowl. Stir with a whisk, spatula, or spoon to thoroughly stir / mix the ingredients. do not whip or add air. Pour into pie shell(s) and bake on a baking sheet in the oven for 1 hr 10 min.

If it has a grainy texture after baking, you have not given enough time in mixing for the sugar to be completely incorporated. Next time mix / stir a little longer.

ETC.

Caramel
(multi-use caramel— not caramel candy)

So many recipes for caramel and everyone promises they have the best one ever. Well, I personally really like this recipe and I doubly like it because it is so easy and fool-proof. Give it a try.

HEAVY SAUCE PAN

1 c butter—room temp
1 c packed light brown sugar
1 c light (clear) corn syrup
1 can sweetened condensed milk
2 T heavy whipping cream
2 t vanilla
1 t salt

Put all top 5 ingredients in the sauce pan on medium heat. Whisk slowly to blend and mix but not to fluff or add air. Be patient and continue to heat and stir until you have bubbles and then big bubbles (I call them Mt. Vesuvius bubbles). If you want thinner caramel (as in a pour-over sauce), remove from heat now. If you want it stiff, let it bubble another minute or so.

When you remove it from the stove, add the vanilla and salt as you blend gently with the whisk.

Let it cool. Using a spatula, transfer it to a covered container (I use a large mason jar so I can loosen it in the microwave to pouring consistency) and store in the refrigerator for up to a few weeks.

This can be poured over ice cream, bread pudding, cakes, or any way that you like to use caramel.

Chocolate Buttercream Frosting

Chocolate frosting is a little more time consuming because ingredients have to be the right temperature for it to completely mix together.

1 1/2 c unsalted butter melted
3/4 c cocoa powder
1/2 t salt
3/4 c half-n-half warmed
1/2 c whole milk warmed
1 t vanilla
Powdered sugar

In a mixing bowl with a paddle, combine the butter, cocoa powder and salt at medium speed. Scrape the sides and bottom with a spatula to fully incorporate the chocolate before moving on.

Add the milk, half-and-half and vanilla. Be sure that the liquids are warm or the chocolate won't mix in completely. Again, stir sides and bottom with a spatula before moving on.

Begin adding the powdered sugar 2 cups at a time, mixing thoroughly on low to medium speed. You'll add less powdered sugar as it begins to thicken. Stop the mixer several times through this process to stir the bottom and sides. It is surprising how much liquid will settle to the bottom and you can end up with an inconsistent frosting.

This is enough to completely cover a 9" 2-layer cake plus extra.

Cream Cheese Frosting

This is just as easy as the white buttercream icing—
with some changes in proportions and ingredients.

1 8-oz pkg cream cheese softened fully to room temp
1 c butter at room temp
1 t vanilla or almond extract
3 T whole milk + 3 T half 'n half warmed
powdered sugar to consistency

Cream the butter and cream cheese til fully mixed and almost fluffy. Add the vanilla and warm milk mixture gradually until smooth.

Begin adding the powdered sugar a cup or so at a time until you reach the consistency you want. Be sure to have a "tighter" frosting with cream cheese as it tends to loosen with time—this means making sure you have added enough powdered sugar.

White Buttercream Frosting
(for cakes / cupcakes / brownies)

Making fresh frosting is the difference between ordinary and special cakes, etc. It is what makes people notice what a great baker you are. You can also save the extra frosting in the refrigerator for a few days to use on other goodies. This is the basic white buttercream frosting which can be amended for other flavors—noted at the end of the recipe.

> 1 1/2 c butter softened
> 1 t vanilla (or almond)
> 1/2 t salt
> 3 oz warm whole milk
> 2 oz warm half-and-half
> Powdered sugar

Put the butter, vanilla, salt and milk/half 'n half in a mixing bowl with a paddle. Add a couple of cups of powdered sugar. Turn the mixer on the slowest speed to keep the powdered sugar from going every where.

Continue to add some powdered sugar—turning the mixer off for each addition. The quantity of powdered sugar depends on the humidity, butterfat content, and moisture level of other ingredients. This is a recipe that is perfected by stopping the mixer from time to time, scraping and stirring with a spatula, and testing for spreadable thickness. If it isn't thick enough, it will slide around and not "hold"—but too thick and it will not be spreadable. If you add too much powdered sugar, just add a bit of milk or melted butter and mix well.

ESPRESSO BUTTERCREAM: Steep for 5 minutes finely ground coffee with some boiling water just to cover the grounds plus a little extra. Or you can use a tablespoon or two of espresso powder and about 1/3 c boiling water. Pour the liquid and grounds into a fine mesh strainer. You are hoping for a really strong "coffee". Substitute 3 oz of this "espresso" + 2 oz half and half for the liquid in the above butter cream. Just follow the directions above.

Lula's Lemonade

3 c sugar (or more to taste)
2 c very hot water (or boiling)
2 t ground ginger
3 c real lemon juice
13 c water

Mix the first 3 ingredients to dissolve sugar & allow ginger to steep a bit. Add remaining ingredients...and voila — great lemonade.

Iced Tea

4 tea bags of regular tea
1 tea bag peppermint
1 tea bag raspberry or hibiscus

Steep these together or use a coffee maker placing the bags in the coffee filter. Use a full amount of water. Or put the tea bags in the coffee carafe and fill the coffee maker with water and run it.

Pour into a big pitcher and add water to taste.

Pie Crust

This recipe is consistently requested—and some would have paid for pie crust lessons! It is a "here we go" recipe—one that I find easy to make but only because I have made thousands (literally!). I describe it as equivalent to learning to ride a bike. Be patient—practice helps.

This is not a recipe to be trifled with—follow it with all ingredients because this is an effort to have a tasty, flaky crust that is more heart-healthy than usual and has a marvelous flavor and consistency.

Be sure to use the dough ASAP as it can get too "thick" with gluten formation over time. I tell folks I'm "committing to the crust" and not to interrupt me until I am finished!

2 CRUSTS	4 CRUSTS
3 c all purpose flour	6 c all purpose flour
1 1/2 t salt	1 T salt
3/4 c veg. oil of choice	1 1/2 c veg. oil
3 T vodka	6 T vodka
5 T water	10 T water

rolling pin
bench scraper
scissors
waxed paper

Whisk together flour & salt—really well—needs to be an even mixture.

Add all liquid ingredients at once to flour mix—and stir with a spoon. Stir as little as possible—without mixing well—leaving some flour apparent. If over stirred, gluten begins to form and the crust will be more rubber-like and tough.

Use about a half of the 2 crust mix—or 1/4 of the 4 crust mix—and place between 2 sheets of waxed paper—each a bit longer than the width.

Flatten the dough some and use your hands to make a nice circular disk (like a thin hockey puck) before putting the top waxed paper on the dough.

I use a rolling pin that my grandfather turned for me—made of bois d'arc wood. It is about 18" long and 1 1/2 inches in diameter—a lot like a fat dowel of hard wood and not tapered. Get a woodworking friend to turn one for you of maple or similar wood. (Seal it with mineral oil.)

Roll from the center out in alternating directions toward 12:00, then 6:00, then 3:00, and 9:00. The dough will go where it is pushed—and is easy to form a nice round that is a bit wider than the wax paper. Keep rolling and keeping even thickness. Use a flat hand to scan the dough for even thickness and almost translucent looking.

Use the bench scraper to loosen crust from counter where it exceeded the wax paper. Starting at one corner, slowly peel the top sheet of wax paper off. Holding the underneath wax paper, lift the pie crust and flip it on top of the pie plate (I prefer 9" glass), centering it. Gently remove the remaining paper starting at a corner and trying not to tear the dough.

The goal now is to "fit" the crust down into the sloping sides of the pie plate without stretching it. For this process, lift the edge of the dough and set the crust down into the plate. Continue around the edge...then run your finger around the edge of the crust against the bottom of the pie plate (where the sides meet the bottom)- checking for air bubbles. If you have any bubbles, lift the crust from the edge and let that air out.

Using the scissors, cut the crust with about an inch of overhang beyond the pie plate edge. If this is a single crust pie, fold that edge under (between the pie plate and crust) so that the fold is on the outside edge of the plate. Again, this dough will go where you push it, so you can shift the folded dough to be somewhat even in thickness. Now crimp those edges using "pointer and thumb" on one hand and pointer finger on the other hand. The goal is to place your forefinger on the dough edge and close in with the pointer and thumb of the other hand. Or simply imprint all the way around with a fork.

PIE CRUST

You can use the pie crust now or put one sheet of waxed paper against the crust and freeze it for later use.

Unbaked pie shell	use as is
Partially baked pie shell 10 & 10 crust	350 oven—10 min. with wax paper and dried beans—remove paper and beans and bake 10 more minutes
Baked pie shell 14 & 14	350 oven—14 min. with wax paper and dried beans—remove paper and beans and bake 14 more minutes

Sauces / Dressings

COMEBACK SAUCE: I grew up having this in Mississippi many decades ago—delicious and has a bit of bite to it. Make it ahead by mixing all ingredients and store it in the refrigerator for up to a week.

FYI: I use the chili sauce by Heinz—and often substitute brown or other mustard.

              1 c mayonnaise   1 t Worcestershire
              1/4 c chili sauce   1 t black pepper
              1/4 c catsup   2 T minced onion
              1 t creole mustard   2 cloves minced garlic
              1/4 c vegetable oil   2 t Sriracha

AVOCADO-CILANTRO (OR PARSLEY) DRESSING: great on quesadillas, or power bowl, or salads. Blend/process everything together and store in the refrigerator for up to a week.

              1 avocado   2 small cloves garlic chopped
              1/2 c plain Greek yogurt   1 t salt
              1 c water   lime juice—one big squeeze
              2 c cilantro chopped stems and all

GARLIC PARMESAN SAUCE: Such a treat with all the delicious flavors of the herbs and spices. I'm also a big proponent of using Parmesan. Bake the cloves of garlic and olive oil for 25 min. in a 350 oven wrapped in foil. Cool and mash them well. Add all ingredients in a food processor and mix until smooth. Refrigerate this sauce overnight and begin using the following day.

              6 cloves garlic   1/2 t kosher salt
              1 T olive oil   1/2 t crushed red pepper
              1/2 c mayonaise   1/4 t dried oregano
              1 t sugar   1/4 t dried basil
              2 - 3 T parmesan   1/4 t black pepper

SAUCES / DRESSINGS

1 T apple cider vinegar
1 t lemon juice

1/8 t dried thyme

CHAMPAGNE VINAIGRETTE: We had daily requests for this recipe. It is such a light and flavorful salad dressing. A tip for serving this is to put dressing around the edges of the bowl and add the greens to the bowl and stir. This keeps the dressing from commanding the salad but allows the flavors to elevate the greens.

1/2 c champagne vinegar
1 c light olive oil
3 T honey
3 T dijon mustard
3 buds roasted garlic
1/4 t Herbs de Provence
1/8 t thyme
1/8 t crushed red pepper
1/8 t salt
1/8 t pepper

Use an immersion blender or food processor/blender to combine all ingredients. Taste the dressing and add more herbs and spices to taste. Store the dressing in the refrigerator—and count on people wanting your recipe!

Woofies (Dog Treats)

This was such a surprise—we offered these on a whim and dogs LOVED them. Owners ordered 12 dozen or more at a time. Some told us they'd buy the cookbook just to get this recipe as their dogs began only accepting these! We often shipped these out of state...wow (or perhaps bow-wow).

PREHEAT OVEN TO 350 DEGREES

6 c whole wheat flour
1 1/2 c dry milk powder
2 eggs
1 c vegetable oil
Beef or chicken soup base (comes in a plastic jar)
or powdered bouillon—a couple of heaping tablespoons will do
1 1/2 c warm water (to dissolve the above beef/chicken)
4 T brown sugar or 3 heaping spoonfuls

Combine all ingredients.

Knead by hand 1 minute—til no longer so sticky

Roll out on floured surface to about 1/4 to 3/8 inch thick—doesn't really matter as your dog isn't that particular!

Cut with dog bone shaped cutter—or any shape you prefer. Place these close together on a large parchment covered baking sheet. You can "fork mark" the center of each if you like that look (again—the dogs don't care!).

Bake 30 minutes—cool. These can also be frozen once baked. They make great holiday gift bags for friends with dogs.

Index

Index

Baked Oatmeal 15
Banana Bread 17
Biscuits 19
Biscuits - Quick & Easy 21
Blueberry Pie 57
Bread Pudding 58
Breads:
    Banana Bread 17
    Zucchini Bread 34
Breakfast Bar 22
Breakfast Cookie 23
Breakfast Pie 25
Brownies 59
Buttermilk Pie 63
Buttermilk Pound Cake 65
Cakes:
    Buttermilk Pound Cake 65
    Carrot Cake 67
    Chocolate Cake 73
    German's Chocolate Cake 84
    Italian Cream Cake 87
    Red Velvet Cake 99
    White Cake 101
Caramel
Carrot Cake 67
Cherry Pie 68
Chocolate Chip Cookies 69
Chocolate Cake 73
Cinnamon Rolls 27
Coconut Cream Pie 75
Cream Cheese Frosting 110

French Silk Pie 79
Frosting
    Chocolate Buttercream 109
    Cream Cheese 110
    White Buttercream 111
Fudge Pie 83
German's Chocolate Cake 84
Gluten Free:
    Baked Oatmeal 15
    Breakfast Bar 22
    Hummus 38
    Power Bowl 43
Hummus 38
Italian Cream Cake 87
Key Lime Pie 91
Lemonade - Tea 112
Oatmeal / Baked 15
Oatmeal Chocolate Chip Cookies 93
Oatmeal Raisin Cookies 94
Peanut Butter Crunch Pie 95
Pecan Pie 97
Pie Crust 113
Pies:
    Blueberry Pie 57
    Breakfast Pie 25
    Buttermilk Pie 63
    Cherry Pie 68
    French Silk Pie 79
    Fudge Pie 83
    Key Lime Pie 91
    Peanut Butter Crunch Pie 95

INDEX

Pecan Pie 97
Pumpkin Pie 98
Tomato Pie 53
Wicked Pie 103
Pimiento Cheese 39
Potato Corn Chowder 40
Power Bowl 43
Pumpkin Pie 98
Quesadillas 47
Quiche 49
Red Velvet Cake 99
Sauces / Dressings
    Avocado Cilantro Sauce 116
    Caramel Sauce 108
    Come Back Sauce 116
    Garlic Parmesan 116
Scones 33
Scones: Cranberry-orange 31
Tomato Pie 53
Vegan:
    Chocolate Cake 73
    Blueberry Pie 57
    Hummus 38
    Power Bowl 43
White Cake 101
Wicked Pie 103
Woofies (dog treats) 118
Zucchini Bread 34

Photo by James Grayson, Go Texas Productions, LLC

Notes

Notes

www.ingramcontent.com/pod-product-compliance
Lightning Source LLC
Chambersburg PA
CBHW042055050526
44107CB00110B/1190